York City Memoirs

YORK CITY FC

Compiled by Garry Vaux

York City Memoirs

Published in Great Britain by GJB Publishing
ISBN: 9780956334336

GJB Publishing
18 Yeend Close, West Molesey, Surrey KT8 2NY
www.GJBpublishing.co.uk   feedback@GJBpublishing.co.uk

Contents

Dedication

This book is dedicated to Graham Bradbury, a true York City fanatic through to the bone, without whose help, cajoling, and valued friendship this book would not have been possible, and would also be a lot thinner!

Foreword

It has been my great joy – the cynics might have a different opinion! – to follow the fortunes of York City over some six decades.

My father took me to my first match in 1941 when I stood at the Grosvenor Road end, which was then, unlike today, the home end, although in those days remember supporters of the two clubs were happy to mix without any problem.

Later I became the City reporter for the *Evening Press* while for the past seven years I have covered games for the *Yorkshire Post* – some 1,600 games in total.

Clearly we all have great memories of the glory days watching City and it is important that those memories are not allowed to disappear into the distance without any record being kept.

It is for this reason that I am delighted to know that Garry has worked hard in getting a wide cross section of players to write down their memories for the benefit of others in this lovingly prepared book.

I hope that readers will get as much pleasure as I did in sharing those memories.

Malcolm Huntington MBE

Introduction

York City Football Club has had many highs and lows since its formation in 1922 – epic cup runs, thrilling promotions and heart-breaking relegations – and every City fan will have their own personal memories.

You can now re-live those memories through the eyes of a host of former 'Minstermen' including 10 former Clubmen of the Year.

Covering 7 decades of City's history, this unique collection will give you a fascinating insight into the club during different eras and will evoke plenty of memories, both happy and sad.

A lot of things have happened to the club since this book was first published on 2001 – unfortunately mostly bad and reading some of the contributions now, you can see where some of the seeds were being sown.

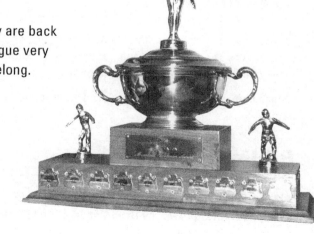

Let's hope that City are back in the Football League very soon, where we belong.

Garry Vaux

February 2011

Acknowledgments

I would like to thank the Evening Press, Newsquest (York) Ltd. for the use of their photographic library, Graham Bradbury, Dave Stanford, Trish Westland, Geoff Saunders, Richard Wright, Gordon Byrne, Dave Batters, Hull City FC and Walsall FC for their help in making this possible.

Disclaimer

The views expressed in this book are those of the individual contributors and not of the author and should be taken in the good spirit in which they are intended.

Please note: some of the language used in this book is of a 'colourful' nature.

Bibliography

"*York City – A Complete Record*" by Dave Batters
"*Citizens & Minstermen*" by Dave Windross and Martin Jarred
www.soccerbase.com

the *1930s*

Dando Fulfordgate 30-3

7-38 *Hath*

Baines 37 193 1937

32 Quarter-finals

1933 3

pooner

Bootham Crescent 193

1934 193

35 Jock Coll

F.A. Cup 31-32

Division 3 (North)

Pinder 19

Having formed in 1922, it was only 7 years later that York City entered the Football League. The club played at Fulfordgate on the outskirts of the City, and the seeds of the club's traditions were being sown.

It wasn't long until some players began to etch their names in the clubs folklore.

There was striker Reg Baines who, in two spells, notched up 86 goals in 121 games, including 29 League goals in his first two seasons (a record that stood for 20 years) and 7 League hat-tricks.

Albert Thompson scored 28 goals in his one and only season with the club and Maurice Dando hit the net 46 times in 86 appearances. Not to mention the likes of Peter Spooner, Harold Beck, Ted Wass, Sam Earl and Jack Pinder, who all gave excellent service to the club.

In 1932, City moved to their current home at Bootham Crescent. The club were having moderate League success but it was in the F.A. Cup where City were making a name for themselves.

In 1936-37 City reached the 4th round and went out in a replay, and the following season they went on an epic run, reaching the quarter-finals, knocking out Coventry City, West Brom (with a Reg Baines hat-trick) and Middlesbrough along the way, eventually going out to Huddersfield Town in a replay in front of 58,000.

Jack Pinder *(Right Back)*

1932-48 • 221 games • 4 goals
F.A. Cup Quarter finals 1937-38

I attained schoolboy honours in 1926-27, playing for England against Wales at Bristol Rovers' ground, and captaining England against Scotland at Hampden Park.

I joined York City at the age of 15 in 1928 and my career ended in 1948.

We played at Fulfordgate at the time, and it was a lovely surface to play on, never got heavy even if it had rained for hours, real springy turf. The crowd in those days was about 3-4,000.

On January 11th 1929 City played Newcastle United in a F.A. Cup tie. The crowd was 12,583. Newcastle won 2-1 with Hugh Gallacher scoring the winning goal.

Local players trained at night at Fulfordgate, two lights in the stand lit up one side of the ground and the lights from Fulford College helped along the other side.

In 1930-31 City again reached the 3rd round of the F.A. Cup, playing against Sheffield United. City drew 1-1 at Bramhall Lane but United won the replay at Fulfordgate 2-0. A record crowd of 12,721 attended the match.

Jock Collier was the manager at the time. The first two players of any note to come from League football to join us were Tom McDonald and Joe Harris from Newcastle. I played behind him when I was 16 and he taught me quite a lot.

I am almost sure Barrow were the first club of the Northern Section to visit Fulfordgate.

In 1937-38 City reached the sixth round of the F.A. Cup and I took my place in all the rounds. The team was; Wharton, Pinder, Barret, Duckworth (captain), Wass, Hathway, Earl, Hughes, Baines, Comrie and Spooner.

City were eventually beaten in a replay by Huddersfield at Bootham Crescent in front of 28,123, still a club record.

During the 1941-42 war-time season there were several notable guest players. Sam Bartram, 'Sailor' Brown, Tom Dawson (Charlton), Raich Carter (Sunderland), Dixie Dean (Everton) and Leslie Compton (Arsenal) all wore City's colours.

City competed in the Combined Counties Cup during the War and we beat Chesterfield, Halifax, Huddersfield, Bradford and Middlesbrough, however the best War-time run was in 1942-43 when we reached the Northern Semi-final. I played in all the matches with Sam Gledhill and George Lee (who was transferred to West Bromwich and won a Cup Winners medal with them).

After my playing days I scouted for the club for a few years. I enjoyed every minute at York City and had many happy years with the club.

Jack Pinder

the *1940s*

With the outbreak of World War Two the Football League closed down, but regional competitions took place and a lot of famous 'guest' players donned City's colours; Bert 'Sailor' Brown, Hughie Gallagher, Raich Carter, Sam Bartram and Everton legend 'Dixie' Dean.

During this time, York-born George Lee was prolific and scored over 100 goals for the club. He reached his milestone with a penalty in a second leg tie of the Football League War Cup semi-final in 1943. A fine achievement by player and club considering the coming and going of players during this time.

City did pick up some silverware two seasons earlier when they won the Combined Counties Cup beating Halifax in the final of this regional competition.

With the resumption of League competition in 1946 it was a time for reconstruction of the City side and 34 players were used in that first peace time season.

Among the City team were local lad Alf Patrick, Matt Patrick (no relation), Jimmy Rudd and Bert Brenan who all gave the club great service.

John Simpson became York's first £1,000 signing in 1948 and George Lee was sold for a then record of £7,500 to Nottingham Forest.

City's League success was moderate but attendances were on the increase and the 1948-49 season saw City have average home gates of over 10,000.

Alf Patrick *(Forward)*
1946-53 • 241 games • 117 goals

During my career with York City I had quite a few memorable times.

The one that gives me the most pleasure was the 5 goals I scored in the 6-1 win over Rotherham United. They were the Division 3 leaders at the time and it was played before 20,000 fans at Bootham Crescent.

I also remember scoring two goals in a 3-2 win away to Hull, who had Raich Carter, the ex-Sunderland and England International in their side as player-manager. He was everywhere, taking throw-ins, corners, free-kicks, the lot! With about 20 minutes to go we were 2-0 down and then I scored twice and George Ivey got the third and we'd won in front of 42,000 spectators.

I was the first City player to score 100 League goals for the club in peace time and in my 8 year career at York scored 117 goals in 241 games, averaging a goal every other game.

Jimmy Rudd was on of the best players I ever played with and he was a real character. We were playing at Accrington Stanley and Jimmy wasn't bothering too much and at half-time Tom Lockie, who was manager at the time, tore Jimmy off a strip.

In those days there was always a brass band playing at half-time and when the game restarted some members of the band used to go round the touch line often holding a large sheet in which spectators used to throw coins in to support the band. Well we looked round and there was Jimmy picking coins up off the pitch, this was with the game in progress!

It seems such a long time ago now and people have since passed my goals total, but the 5 goals I scored against Rotherham still stands as a record after 50 years.

Cyril Coultate *(Right Winger)*
1942 • 1 game • 0 goals

The manager then was Tom Lockie, and he saw me on leave from the army just before Christmas 1942. He told me he was looking for players to make up the team for the Christmas Day match at Rotherham as some of his forces regulars were going home for Christmas.

The team travelled by train to Rotherham and I remember Tom coming round on the way giving out chicken sandwiches to everybody.

It was an honour to play in the same team as Sam Bartram and "Sailor" Brown, both characters and England stars and, though the match was played at a much faster pace than I was used to, I remember rounding the full-back and providing the centre for our centre-forward, Christopher Marshall, to head in our second goal. We lost 3-2 in front of a 6,000 crowd.

Getting off the train at York, Tom gave me a 10 shilling note to "buy my tea" with. So ended a memorable day.

the *1950s*

City had a new manager in Dick Duckworth, having taken over from Tom Mitchell, Alf Patrick continued his goalscoring feats, and he was joined by Billy Fenton who, in his first season, notched 31 League goals to set a new club record.

The most outstanding feat of this time was when City shocked the footballing world by reaching the semi-finals of the F.A. Cup in 1954-55, knocking out Blackpool, Tottenham and Notts County before going out to eventual winners Newcastle United after taking them to a replay.

This was arguably City's best ever side and had so many quality players amongst its ranks; Arthur Bottom, who in his first season equalled Fenton's 31 goal haul, goalkeeper Tommy Forgan, Ernie Phillips, George Howe, Gordon Brown, Alan Stewart, Ron Spence, Norman Wilkinson, Billy Fenton, Sid Storey and Billy Hughes. This team was nicknamed the 'Happy Wanderers' and won many plaudits for the quality of their play. Even more remarkable was that for the majority of the season they played without a manager.

The following season they reached the 4th round of the Cup and Arthur Bottom hit another 31 League goals, and he again made headlines in 1957 when, with his 4 goals, City recorded their record win, a 9-1 victory over Southport.

1958-59 saw City finish 3rd in the newly formed Division 4 and record their first promotion under the captaincy of Peter Wragg.

Sid Storey *(Midfield)*

1947-56 • 354 games • 42 goals
F.A. Cup semi finals 1954-55

I spent 9 years at York City and enjoyed my time there.

My most memorable time was during 1954-55 when we reached the semi-final of the F.A. Cup.

The most memorable matches were beating Blackpool 1-0 and playing against Stanley Matthews, and the match against Tottenham at Bootham Crescent when Danny Blanchflower was captain.

As I was only a part-time player I didn't see what happened during the week, only on Saturday, but I am sure it was a happy club.

S Storey

Margo Fenton *wife of the late*
Billy Fenton *(Left winger)*
1951-58 • 278 games • 124 goals
F.A. Cup semi-finals 1954-55

After leaving a modern semi with a garden in Blackburn to find our home in York was to be an old terrace house with no bathroom or hot water, a yard and outside toilet, I was a bit disappointed. Bill always looked on the bright side so we took a positive outlook and things seemed better.

Mr Kitchin, the then chairman, and a true gentleman, came to visit after a couple of days to welcome us personally which gave us a good feeling.

When we left that house in Heslington Road after seven happy years to move to our own modern semi with a garden (full circle!) I shed a few tears to be leaving a sunny, friendly house and many good friends and neighbours.

Dick Duckworth was the manager who signed Bill, and before many many games he would say "We have a bit of a game on here today Bill. Now the full back against you is a bit thick about the hips and slow on the turn, so you'll have a field day against him."…..Not always so!!!

One memorable game was against Carlisle. City were 4-1 down at half-time but came out winners 5-4, Bill scoring 4 and Norman Wilkinson the other.

Of course the 1955 Cup run was where Bill Fenton on the left flank was very fast, direct and had a good eye for goal. Arthur Bottom, or "Nodder" as the lads called him was a great striker of a dead ball and a scorer of fantastic goals. Sid Storey was an excellent ball playing inside left with exceptional passing

ability. Last but not least, Norman Wilkinson, an experienced centre forward, good all round ability and very unselfish.

Those lads played as a team, no egos no stars, just played for each other and enjoyed their football!

I often wonder what Bill would think of the game now. There has been a lot of changes in 28 years.

Margo Fenton

Gordon Brown *(Midfield)*
1950-58 • 351 games • 25 goals
F.A. Cup semi-finals 1954-55

I joined York from Notts Forest in 1950, Mr. Dick Duckworth was the manager, a very straight forward man, what we called in the old days, a player's man. He'd give you a good rollicking but after it was finished, he never held a grudge.

One amusing story I can remember was when we played a six-a-side match, Ron Spence and myself were on the same side, the manager was the ref, and our side were getting beaten, which didn't go down very well with Ron and myself. We had a few bust ups about how he was refereeing the match, anyway, it got that heated that he blew the whistle for time.

We got back to the ground, and Tom Lockie the trainer said "Gordon and Ron, the boss wants to see you in his office when you're changed." We went down to his office and knocked. "Come in" he said. He was standing in front of his desk, he pointed to his chair, "sit down", so Ron sat down. "Alright?" he asked, "fine" said Ron. "Would you like to try it Gordon?", so I sat down. "You might as well stay there because you two have more mouth than I have."

He gave us a good rollicking then kicked us out of the office, but the next day it was as if nothing had happened. I bumped into him as I came in for training the next day "Good morning Gordon", "Good morning boss". That was the sort of man he was.

What we had at York in those days was team spirit, right down from the chairman, the directors, the training staff, players, groundsman, supporters, everybody were mates.

I'd like to mention two of the Directors, Mr D. Blundy and Mr. A. Brown, everyone at the club had a lot of respect for these two gentlemen. Mr Arthur Brown is still seen at the club, sadly Mr Blundy passed away.

I would like to mention that one of the fondest memories I have happened a couple of years ago at Steve Tutill's testimonial dinner. Graham Bradbury organised it, all the players who had played 350 games or more were invited, as was the cup side of 1955. We were all presented with a framed photo of all the players, the number of games each player had played, and the years each one had spent at the club. That is one of my fondest memories, thank you (Graham Bradbury).

The matches I remember most were those played in the F.A. Cup run of 1955, and the one that stands out was the one game Tottenham in the 5th round.

The semi-final was special, but the Tottenham game was something else. The weather that week was bad, we had snow and ice and it took all week to get the ground fit to play on. Everybody gave a hand, even the supporters mucked in cleaning the snow and ice, and then to beat them 3-1 was great!

Gordon Brown

Everybody played well but Norman Wilkinson, our centre forward, was outstanding. One of the goals he scored was a header, one of the best I've seen.

In those days, we didn't have a squad of players where you can take one player off and replace them with another. You played our best eleven, and that eleven started and finished the match.

At York from 1953 to 1957 it was practically the same side, the only time changes were made were for injuries.

I can honestly say that I can never remember anybody having a cross word, the team played for each other, that was the secret of our success.

Gordon Brown

Norman Wilkinson *(Forward)*

1954-66 • 401 games • 143 goals (club record)
F.A. Cup semi-finals 1954-55
Promotion 1958-59 & 1964-65

We lost our manager in 1954 but still finished 4th in the League. In the F.A. Cup we nearly made it to Wembley, losing after a replay at Roker Park to Newcastle United in the semi-final. Maybe we could have won the game at Hillsborough but for a late goal line clearance.

In 1955-56, because the team spirit and the balance of the side was so good, it almost picked itself. In the Cup we went out in round 4 losing to Sunderland in a replay at Roker Park, on a snow cleared pitch on a very cold day. Some of the Sunderland players wore gloves and Len Shackleton wore his stockings all the way up his legs. 4 of the team were part-timers, only meeting the other players on match days.

The following season, having beaten Birmingham in the 3rd round, we went out to the eventual winners Bolton Wanderers in a replay. They went on to beat Manchester United. In February, Arthur Bottom was transferred to Newcastle United, where he scored 10 goals in 11 matches, which many people thought helped keep them up, only to be released at the end of the season, moving to Chesterfield.

In 1958-59 the club finished 3rd in the 4th division, winning promotion. The following year was not very good, finishing 21st in Division 3.

In 1960-61 we finished 5th in Division 4, but again the Cup saw us replaying with Bradford, Tranmere and Norwich, losing to the latter through a very late penalty.

Norman Wilkinson

We had a good Cup run in 1961-62, this time in the League Cup, being beaten in the Fourth round. We had played Leicester City, who included Gordon Banks and Frank McLintock, and Watford who had Tommy Hamer. In the League we went down one position.

The following season was not a very good year, losing 0-5 to Southampton, our only game for 10 weeks due to the weather!

In 1963-64 we finished 22nd having lost 2-5 to Carlisle, but the following season was a good year, winning promotion, finishing 3rd in the 4th Division.

My last season was 1965-66, only managing to play 4 games.

After retiring at York, I played a little Sunday football with friends, who in their wisdom converted me to centre half. However in my last match, I was converted back to centre forward and managed to score a hat-trick. I also played a few games for Annfield Plain, where I started my career, and still help out, one time playing for them in an emergency forward line. Average age – 52 years!

Norman F Wilkinson

Colin Addison *(Forward)*

1957-61 • 97 games • 31 goals
Promotion 1958-59

Amongst my most memorable games was the game versus Newcastle played to open the new floodlights at Bootham Crescent. The game finished York 2 Newcastle 8. The Newcastle team was captained by Jimmy Scoular and included Bobby Mitchell and Ivor Allchurch amongst others.

My last game for York was at Norwich in an F.A.Cup replay, we lost 1-0. Walter Bingley gave away a last minute penalty.

George Teasdale was secretary, Tom Lockie was the trainer – a very hard scotsman, Sam Bartram, the manager who signed me as a professional. The groundsman was a great friend – Bryan Foster – who used to play with me in the youth team.

I played with the likes of Barry Jackson, Ken Boyes, Ron Mollatt, Micky Granger, George Howe and Peter Wragg, who helped me get interested in coaching. My first session being at Ampleforth College. Whilst managing Scarborough I saw a lot of Ken Boyes who lives in the town, we have always kept in touch over the years.

My debut game was against Bury at Bootham Crescent in September 1957. The team was Forgan, Phillips, Howe, Brown, Cairney, Wragg, Hughes, Bottom, Wilkinson, Addison, Fenton and we won 2-1 with goals from Bottom & Fenton.

It's a great little club with some wonderful memories.

Colin Addison

Mick Granger *(Goalkeeper)*
1951-62 • 81 games

I was at Bootham Crescent for 10 years and enjoyed every minute. I suppose my two most noteworthy games were against QPR and Birmingham. We drew 0-0 at Loftus Road when they were going for the League title, and beat Birmingham 3-1 in the F.A. Cup at Bootham Crescent when they had about 6 internationals in their side.

In my time at City I can't think of any player or member of staff that I disliked. There were some great characters but Barry Jackson stood out. He was a big man with a big heart and way out in most things he did. He was a great centre half to play behind in goal, and how he didn't go on to bigger things is beyond me. There was also Gordon Brown who was a brilliant wing half with a great sense of humour.

"Forgie" (Tommy Forgan) was a superb 'keeper, my so called rival, but I will remember him as a very good friend. Gus Alexander, was a fine inside forward with great one-liners that never failed to make me laugh.

Among the backroom staff at the time were Tom Lockie, trainer and later manager, Sid Storey, trainer and a great inside forward in his day, Sam Johnstone, trainer and Billy Sherrington, every one of them gave me great help in my early days and I appreciate their help to this day.

Wragg

66-67

jackson

the *1960s*

1963

promo

AiMSON

66

64-65

1962

967

Addison

L'ockie

60-61

1968

1965

MacDo

Provan

196

63-64

61-62

62

961

re-elections

After being relegated back to Division 4, City once again pushed for promotion.

Whilst striving for success they reached the 5th round of the recently introduced League Cup, knocking out First Division Leicester City along the way.

After finishing 22nd in 1963-64 under Tom Lockie, City turned it around the following season. Lockie brought in Andy Provan and Paul Aimson, who went on to net over 100 goals for City, and with their help and the backbone of Tommy Heron, Alan Woods, Barry Jackson, Dennis Walker, veteran Norman Wilkinson and skipper Billy Rudd, City finished 3rd in the division, scoring 91 League goals, winning 7 consecutive league games (a club record) and winning 20 of their 23 home games (another club record).

Unfortunately City were relegated the following season and over the next few years City's League form slumped.

Goalkeeper Tommy Forgan made the last of his 428 appearances and among the stars of the time were Dave Dunmore, Eamon Dunphy, Tommy Spencer, Ken Turner and Phil Boyer and Ted MacDougall, who were forming a fruitful partnership which would serve them both well together at other clubs.

The club had to apply for re-election on three successive occasions, but from these dark times City would go on to reach new heights.

Barry Jackson *(Centre Half)*

1956-70 • 539 games (club record) • 10 goals
Promotion 1958-59 & 1964-65

York City AFC meant everything to me until I was 31 years old. Playing the best football of my career in that last season, never out of the first team, when cruel circumstances (not entirely of my own doing) brought my career to an abrupt end.

In retrospect, after a lot of heartache, it was a good way to go. My life without football has been much more varied and happy. It enables me not to be so narrow in my thinking because York City always came first.

With regard to memorable games they all were for me personally. Everytime I pulled on a York City shirt meant everything to me and money didn't come into it!! The game has gone money mad and is a lot worse for it!

I joined the club when they were on the crest of a wave, the year after getting to the semi-finals of the F.A. Cup. From then on there was highs and lows throughout. I played with all the semi-final team and they were all wonderful to me. I could not have been encouraged and cajoled more. I do think players in my day at the club were in general a very happy lot even when we were struggling. We even took temporary employment in the summer together (painting houses in New Earswick) to eke the summer wage out!!

Looking from the outside into the club as it stands now, there are a lot more staff with players thinking of themselves first (which they have to contractually). It's a different game money wise. Players ending their careers now must find great difficulty adjusting to normal wages if they need to!! This is not sour grapes just a realistic statement. It is not the players fault, it's the system.

The club has always been well run but I think it is even better run now. Tremendous training ground, great youth policy. The board is not at all that bad.

Despite the rhetoric about this new contractual system I think York City can make it work better for themselves. In the position they are in now, if it comes off, York City should concentrate more than ever on youth. The Club must not let really promising young players go too early. I still think the young players they have let go lately, Greening, Cresswell, Culkin, should have been kept for at least two or three years more and York City would have had the benefit.

When players leave York they should move straight into the relevant first team. It is no good to them or York City becoming Player of the Year in Manchester United's second team. It does not mean a thing. First team football is what matters, be it Premier or Third Division. Second team football means nothing!! It's a runout, nothing else!

Back room staff are very important, they are the backbone of the club.

Barry Jackson

Mr. Sherrington, secretary for years, Tom Lockie, trainer, manager and physio at one time (these salaries now!!) Bryan Foster, terrific character, great groundsman. I appreciate these people more than ever after supporting my wife Susan for two years through a Management Degree course at 48 years of age. She finished at 50 and they were without doubt the hardest 2 years of our married life, and it really made me appreciate how important the back room staff are!! Tears rolled down my cheeks when she received her Degree at Leeds Town Hall.

The fans are the absolute heart and soul of the club. In my time and after, there have been people who have just about devoted themselves to the club. Their only reward, success when it

Barry Jackson

comes. Terrific! I think the idea of representation at Board meetings from the Supporters Club is a great idea.

There were many amusing stories but I will just quote one.

Early in the 1958-59 season we played Torquay home and away, both midweek evening games and we stayed overnight in Torquay. It was always difficult to sleep after a night game so all the team went out for a drink together. When playing Monday or Tuesday there wasn't another game until Saturday so we all finished in a night club. Also in the night club was Tommy Cooper who was appearing in Torquay for the summer season.

Tommy Heron, our Scottish full back, was a real character. When he had a drink he often swore like a trooper and nobody understood him!! He started shouting "Come on Tommy, give us a turn!" Eventually Tommy got up (shouldn't have done under contract to another company) and brought the house down. He gave us all a great evening. Incidentally, there was a small dance square and I have never seen anybody as tall with such big feet be so light on those feet!!

In conclusion, there is nothing more I would like to see than York City progress through the League with 5 or 6 players that have come up through the Youth teams. Dreams for the future.

Barry Jackson

Phil Burrows *(Left Back)*

1966-74 • 390 games • 15 goals
Promotion 1970-71 & 1973-74
Clubman of the Year 1973-74

No one warned me about what to expect when I entered the dressing room at Bootham Crescent in the summer of 1966 when, as a very immature 20 year old, I signed from the shadows of Manchester City reserves. To say that it was a shock to the system would be an understatement.

The dressing room door burst open and in strode this ginger haired colossus with a smile, laugh and personality that would frighten any opponent (and it did, believe me! – Just ask John Toshack!)

Barry Jackson! 'Jacko'! 'The Big Fella'! York City's very own superstar. I would become his defensive partner for a number of seasons and my good friend took me under his wing.

He not only reinforced my philosophy of how the games should be played, but showed by example how a "so called" veteran should train and remain at the peak of fitness and form, he became the second biggest influence in my career following my own father's skill, experience and encouragement.

We would go for a walk around the city centre and I would be totally amazed by the number of people who would acknowledge his presence. Mind you, you could hardly miss him, could you?!

We would also train together. Imagine the situation – Little Nipper at 5 feet 8 inches and 10 stone and "Jacko" at 6 feet 3 inches, and a damn sight heavier – practising tackling! As a natural left sided player, I could hold my own tackling with my favoured foot, but on my weaker foot, with this guy who doesn't know how to hold back, I can still feel the shock waves reverberating through my body to this day!!

I made many friends during my stay at City including Roly Horrey, the flying right winger. Roly and Denise looked after me during our one season together at York.

Phil Boyer moved into my old digs with landlady Ol Simpson in 1968. Every Friday, he came for a meal at my own home, and during our trip to the supermarket with "Charlie" Boyer in tow, my wife Elizabeth and myself would find all kinds of rubbish thrown in our basket and we spent, what seemed like hours finding what shelf Llama's testicles in Spew Sauce came from. If you ever wanted to test your fitness, try marking this bundle of energy during a game, especially on the sandy pitch at the end of a long season!!

Ron Hillyard was also a good friend and I was grateful to Ron and his wife who allowed me to stay at their home during my month's loan at Gillingham. Despite his boyish looks, he was as hard as nails, and we both enjoyed our friendly skirmishes in five-a-side games.

Chris Topping, YCFC's first apprentice, and an absolute gentleman footballer. Mr. "Perpetual Motion" – it became hard graft staring at his backside, miles in the distance on endurance runs.

John Stone and John Mackin were also close friends along with a host of others.

Last, but my no means least is my old mate Graeme Crawford, my buddy and room mate. Our goalkeeper extraordinaire, deservedly equalled the Football League record of 11 games without conceding a goal in the 1973-74 season. During this run, apparently, our opponents were awarded 9 penalties and

Phil Burrows

missed them all, according to Graeme (but I can't remember him saving any!!?!)

There were some highs and lows in my time at City, the ultimate low was beginning my Football League career with York City and having to apply for re-election for three consecutive seasons.

The obvious highs were to be in the side which took York City into the old Second Division for the first time in the club's history and also, personally, becoming the first player to receive the "Clubman of the Year" on the day we achieved promotion, from Mrs Margo Fenton, the famous Billy Fenton's widow.

The older fans who can recall this game may also remember the sheer joy (!) of Chairman Bob Strachan and manager Tom Johnston. The manager announced my award in the dressing room and then kept the players inside before sending me out to receive this award alone.

I walked into the players' tunnel, to be met by Chairman Strachan who thrust a microphone into my hand, leaving me without saying a word, to announce myself. Oh, to be popular with the club's officials!

In an eight year career at one club, a whole range of characters pass through. People like Billy Hodgson, a jovial Scot, who made training a joy. Laurie Calloway, who perhaps wasn't at his best at York City, but a very talented footballer nevertheless.

Two people who were at the club all too short a time were Manager Joe Shaw and coach Billy Horner.

Joe Shaw took over from Tom Lockie and brought a lot of modern coaching techniques to the club but business difficulties unfortunately forced him to resign.

Phil Burrows

Billy Horner came as a coach in the early 70's and as most of us had played against him, he fitted in extremely well. We all had so much respect for him that he was treated as one of the lads, but when Bill said 'Work' everyone would knuckle down.

His frustrating spell at City came to end, when he was denied the team sheet by the manager, on a Friday morning, denying him the opportunity of working with selected players on set pieces etc ready for the next day's game. The team sheet would be pinned on the notice board, in the dressing room whilst we were out training.

Finally, despite all the highs and lows, the frustrating and annoying attempts at contract negotiations with a dour and irritating Scot, the appaling unhygenic conditions within the changing rooms causing numerous infections as well as other personal discontent resulting in a players' revolt in the early 70's, my career with York City (exactly half my career) is still regarded by myself with great affection towards the club, the players and all the supporters.

I really enjoy my return visits to the City (by courtesy of Graeme Crawford and Graham Bradbury) and the recent reunion with the 1973-74 team.

The squad was a team unit in every sense and thoroughly deserved the success it achieved.

Footnote (Left foot, naturally)

The Summerbee family don't have a monopoly on three generations of footballers.

The Burrows family have also produced three. My footballing pedigree has been well documented at YCFC whereas my father and grandfather, both named Arthur, were professionals (both part-time) with amongst other teams, our home town club, Stockport County.

My father also played in the longest ever games, 206 minutes (two and a quarter consecutive games) in March 1946, Stockport County versus Doncaster Rovers. People actually went home for their tea and came back to watch the rest of the game! Barry Swallow's late father, Ernie, also played in this game for Doncaster Rovers.

My grandfather was in the Stockport County 'squad' when the lowest ever attendance at a League Ground (Old Trafford of all places) was recorded, when 13 spectators paid to watch Stockport County play Derby County (I think). The crowd was announced over the loud speaker to the players!! This match was the second game on this particular day and most people watched the two games, but apparently only 13 fans came specifically to watch the second game.

Phil Burrows

Chris Topping *(Centre Half)*

1967-78 • 463 games • 13 goals
Promotion 1970-71 & 1973-74
Clubman of the Year 1974-75

My time at York was a memorable and also a miserable period of my life.

Starting as a 15 year old for York reserves in the Yorkshire League and also on Sunday mornings in a team of youngsters run by Ron Spence, the York trainer.

York is my home club, I was born at Bubwith some 17 miles from the ground and my father's roots were firmly entrenched at York City.

He had been taken down to the Fulfordgate ground by his father who was a committee member there.

Needless to say I jumped at the chance to sign as an apprentice for Tom Lockie, my first manager.

Within six weeks Tom was sacked and Joe Shaw took over. Another six weeks and he had resigned because of his business, a sports shop, and the travelling from Sheffield.

Tom Johnston was to become the next manager, a momentous decision.

When I arrived at York in 1968 players like Barry Jackson, Dennis Walker, Gerry Baker, Phil Burrows and many more were the stars. The team alas was near the bottom of the 4th Division.

Tom Johnston bought wisely, initially Ted McDougall and Phil Boyer were the start of the revival. MacDougall being a proven goalscorer and Boyer his skillful shield. Highlight of these days was the Cup run in which York beat Cardiff of the Second

Division after 2 replays. I will never forget the wonderful sight of Barry Jackson copying the popular song "Jump up and down and wave your knickers in the air" with his jockstrap on his head!

Eventually more players came and others went and we had the basis of that famous team which a lot of people remember:

Morritt/Crawford, Mackin/Stone, Topping, Swallow, Burrows/ Oliver, Lyons, Holmes, Woodward/Lally, Butler, Seal, Jones.

Promotion from the 4th Division came and we then hung on in the 3rd for successive seasons on goal average. The third year we were mid table and feeling safe. We then set off on a run of unbeaten games and clean sheets which was breathless. This was a hard working squad generally, the best of friends who socialised together. They would not give up and, as with all successful teams, had their share of luck.

For a local lad to get promotion twice into the 3rd and 2nd Divisions was a proud moment.

Tom Johnston left at the time which was a blow to myself and the team. His replacement, Wilf McGuiness, was in my view a mistake as Clive Baker, the coach, was more aware of the 2nd

Division and had achieved some excellent results whilst in temporary charge, notably away at Norwich, which we won 3-2 when MacDougall and Boyer played for Norwich.

The 2nd Division was superb and to be presented with the Billy Fenton Trophy for Clubman of the Year was wonderful. Manchester United came and went, again a man of the match trophy. Chelsea, Nottingham Forest and Sunderland were other league visitors.

Other happy memories were being involved in the York v Southampton Cup tie when 3-1 down we drew 3-3 with the famous Paul Aimson header and Arsenal away in the Cup, a 1-1 draw at Highbury. Great days.

Another lasting memory – those famous Y-front shirts being likened to St. Helens by away supporters!

Life after Tom Johnston was fine for a year but then we started a decline ending in McGuiness' dismissal and Charlie Wright being appointed manager.

The club struggled over the next year and eventually I was signed by Tom Johnston for Huddersfield Town in 1978.

York is in my blood, I would love my sons to play for them. We will see!!

Chris Topping

the *1970s*

Under the shrewd management of Tom Johnston, City achieved 2 promotions in 4 seasons to reach what was the old Second Division for the first time in their history.

With the likes of Chris Topping, John Mackin, Phil Burrows, Kevin McMahon, and Barry Swallow they were promoted from Division 4 in 1970-71 including 10 wins in 11 games to help clinch the last promotion spot. Paul Aimson in his second spell at the club, again topped the scoring charts with 31 League and Cup goals.

After consolidation and gradual improvement in the higher division, City, with Graeme Crawford in goal, Brian Pollard and Barry Lyons in midfield and Chris Jones and Jimmy Seal up front, clinched promotion to the Second Division. City's defence of Crawford, John Stone, Phil Burrows, Chris Topping and Barry Swallow went 11 consecutive games without conceding a goal, equalling the Football League record.

City's stay in Division 2 was all too brief. They reached 5th place in the division at one point, their highest ever placing as they played alongside the likes of Manchester United, Sunderland, Bolton Wanderers and Aston Villa, but after only two seasons they were relegated and slid back to the basement division under the management of former 'Busby Babe' Wilf McGuiness.

Graeme Crawford *(Goalkeeper)*

1971-77 & 1980 • 280 games
Promotion 1973-74
11 consecutive clean sheets 1973-74

The most memorable game for me was the very first game in the old Second Division, the opening game against Aston Villa. We knew then that we were in among the big boys. There were some very good teams in that League, Manchester United, Southampton, Villa, Nottingham Forest etc and I believe to this day that had the board had the foresight to look after the manager, the club would have remained there for many seasons.

The appointment of Wilf McGuinness ruined the club as he told us we were not good enough before even giving us a chance. He said he needed to bring his own players in. From the second division to re-election in one easy step.

As a coach Wilf was a great, likeable character but as a manager a total disaster! One story springs to mind. We were training at York University on a really blustery day with Wilf and Clive Baker. During the warm up we were jogging around and the next time we came around Wilf was lying on the ground, prostrate, as if this branch had fallen from the tree and clobbered him. Nobody took any notice of him and we were made to run and run and run because we had not laughed at him, the lads were trying to get away from the re-election zone not watching a bloody comedy act.

The time under Tom Johnston was the most successful time while I was there. Tom was not everybody's cup of tea but he was a shrewd old bugger! Tom's favourite team talk revolved around "you know this team as well as I do, they have been around a long time, go get a result."

John Stone came from Middlesbrough and was making his debut against Portsmouth and Tom decided to boost "Stoney's" confidence. Portsmouth had just signed Peter Marinello (the Scottish George Best) from Arsenal and Tom went into raptures about him, "He jinks this way, he jinks that way, he can play this lad." As he kept enthusing about this you could see "Stoney" sliding further and further down the bench in the dressing room. He was making his debut against this lad and right at the end Tom finished by saying "By the way, he's no' playing". "Stoney" had a stormer!

Graeme

Jimmy Seal *(Forward)*
1972-76 • 183 games • 48 goals
Promotion 1973-74

Life at York City in the early 70's was very exciting. Tom Johnston assembled a team, some players costing money but quite a few on free transfers, but Tom had the knack of assembling a good, balanced, successful team.

My most memorable games were in the F.A. Cup – the two games against Arsenal. The goal I scored at Highbury was a bit special and by the time I got back to York it must have been 45 yards out!

Playing against Manchester City home and away was an experience. They were a top team at the time and Rodney Marsh was very skillful.

Scoring against Manchester United was also very special for me. We put on a good display and deserved a draw.

As individuals we all got on well and had a great time socially. Barry Lyons was a very funny man off the pitch, but on it you respected him for his skill and know-how and Barry Swallow was the best captain I had played for.

Success at York was short and sweet but we had a great time and it was a privilege to play in such a great team.

Neil Warnock *(Winger)*
1978 • 5 games • 0 goals

Unfortunately my time at York City was very short. I signed in the summer for Charlie Wright, and was made captain for the first game. The manager asked me to play even though I was injured – he said it was important. Having been to the doctors on Friday morning, I went to the training ground in my jacket and tie and Charlie asked me to do free kicks and set pieces in the same attire, anyhow I turned out at Grimsby in the League Cup and we lost 2-0.

The following week Charlie called me in and said "You've got critics in the Board room, and I'm going to have to leave you out of the side." You can imagine how I felt with it being the first game of the season, hence that's why Grimsby Town stands out in my memory, and I hardly played a game after that.

Happy memories are of the groundsman, Bryan Foster. He treated his pitches like a woman, and wouldn't let anyone near it, but hence the surface was tremendous!

Kevin Randall *(Centre Forward)*
1977-81 • 118 games • 31 goals

I had some good times at York but obviously it was getting towards the end of my career and my best days were behind me.

I have a few goalscoring memories that stick out in the mind. The first was when I made my debut for City on Friday October 28th 1977, and scored 2 goals at home to Doncaster Rovers.

I also scored 4 goals in the first 3 games of the 1978-79 season including 2 in a thrilling 5-3 victory against Portsmouth. There was also another thrilling 5-3 victory in the F.A.Cup first round replay at Blyth Spartans. I scored one goal, but three of the four Blyth goals were penalties. The result of blatant dives by one of their players, who scored all of them!

During the 1979-80 season I scored in six consecutive games that I played in, the last being in a 5-1 win against Port Vale. Charlie Wright offered me an extra years contract for 1980-81 after the Vale game. I accepted but details were to be formalised the following Monday and in between we played Aldershot away, which was never a lucky ground for me.

I asked Charlie what would happen if I had a bad game. He said it would still be ok. I scored after 2 minutes - securing my contract and scoring in 7 consecutive games.

I was asked to take on the youth coaches role after Charlie Wright left in March 1981 which I accepted, although I continued to play. I then became Barry Lyons assistant in 1981-82 when my mate Dave Pugh left.

Kevin Randall

I made my most significant contribution when I signed Keith Walwyn at the beginning of the 1981-82 season. Keith was a tremendous success, as you know, and many people have tried to claim the credit for signing him. Living in Chesterfield and knowing that scene and regularly watching Chesterfield reserves, I had seen Keith and told Barry Lyons to sign him when we were unsuccessful in signing my old strike partner Ernie Moss.

With respect to Barry he didn't know him. He was however untried and he signed for a year for about £5,000, which was a bit of a gamble for an unproven 24 year old. Barry was away on holiday and I interviewed him and persuaded him to sign.

Barry was asked to stand down and I was requested to take over. I wouldn't take the job without Barry's blessing but he said I should take it on. On Christmas Day 1981 I was rushed to hospital with a perforated appendix, and I came back to work after a week. It was the worst mistake I ever made. I was too weak to work, after losing a stone and a half in weight, and the team eventually had a poor run and I was sacked! Before I left I persuaded Keith Walwyn to sign an extension to his contract.

Goalkeeper Graeme Brown had so many superstitions he had to get to the ground so early to carry them all out. One of them was standing rigid on the penalty spot before kick off. This particular day in the Cup replay at Blyth Spartans there was a couple of minutes delay and the young Blyth supporters pelted "Browny" with snowballs and he never moved!

I remember before one match, as Charlie Wright was giving his team talk, I sensed something was wrong. Peter Lorimer was missing – he was watching the 2.15 race on the TV in the players' lounge!

My experience on the coaching side was a useful exercise in the long term, as at least I learnt how not to do it!

the *1980s*

City started off the 80's by finishing 92nd and bottom of the Football League. Youngsters John Byrne and Gary Ford had broken into the first team and midfielder Ian McDonald was top scorer with 12 League and Cup goals.

The following season saw the arrival of striker Keith Walwyn and he made an immediate impact, scoring 25 League and Cup goals with his powerful forward play.

The club appointed former Stoke stalwart Denis Smith as player manager and with Viv Busby as coach, they dramatically transformed the team.

City picked up the winning habit and made Bootham Crescent a fortress. City acquired Roger Jones in goal, Alan Hay and Ricky Sbragia in defence and Malcolm Crosby in midfield, alongside the established Derek Hood and Brian Pollard, who was in his second spell at City.

After finishing 7th in the Division in 1982-83, City ran away with the championship the following season, rattling up 96 League goals and became the first League club to total over 100 points in a season. Walwyn and Byrne hit 52 goals between them and new signing John MacPhail was a rock in defence.

This was a boom period in City's history and in the coming seasons there were thrilling Cup runs going out to Liverpool in two successive seasons. But the acrimonious departure of Denis Smith signalled a down turn in fortune and the club were soon relegated back to Division 4.

Keith Walwyn *(Forward)*

1981-87 • 291 games • 140 goals
Division 4 Championship 1983-84
Clubman of the Year 1981-82 & 1986-87

My time at York was very enjoyable and all in all everybody got on very well. There was a good banter in the dressing room of which no-one escaped getting the mickey taken out of them, not even Viv Busby and Denis Smith.

I would have to say that John MacPhail usually got ribbed the most for the mirror he carried around with him to check his hair every four minutes, even when he was playing!

One of the most enjoyable characters at the club was the groundsman Bryan Foster ("Fozzy"). He loved horse and dog racing - betting that is - but his biggest love was the turf and if he had had his way there would have been no games played on it at all. If he caught anyone on it, before matchday, there would be a shovel or pitch fork flying towards your head, or he would go sulking in the stands!

Of course the biggest high at the club was when we won the 4th Division championship in 1983-84. Especially when we won it in front of our home fans against Hartlepool.

We had started the season well and our good form just kept going, which resulted in the points and the goals we amassed.

It was also great to beat Arsenal 1-0 in the F.A. Cup. We also had 3 out of 4 good games against Liverpool, one of which we should have won. I'll leave you to decide which one!

Keith Walwyn

John Byrne *(Forward)*
1979-84 • 198 games • 60 goals
Division 4 Championship 1983-84

I signed for the club at the same time as Gary Ford. He was a really big influence on me. He was an absolute stalwart for the club, the "Steady Eddie" on the right! We played for the youth team together and came through the ranks. At the time, City had fallen from the old Second Division and struggling at the bottom of the Fourth Division, the likes of Peter Lorimer and Gordon Staniforth were gracing the City side back then.

I remember my first ever league goal, it was against Scunthorpe at Bootham Crescent, and it was beyond belief! A header! – I rose above everyone to nod it home!

When Denis Smith and Viv Busby took charge, with all due respect to the other people in charge at the time, they knew what they were doing. They knew the players that could get the club out of that division, and the season before the championship you could feel something was going to happen.

I scored the only goal to beat Hull that season in front of nearly 10,000 people at Bootham Crescent. They were going places then and had the likes of Gary Swann, Steve McClaren and Eddie Blackburn in their team. It was the arrival of Smith & Busby that really sparked my career.

My partnership with Keith Walwyn blossomed. I think we were ideal strike partners for each other. Although we were mates off the pitch and socialised together, there was no telepathic link between us. The team as a whole socialised together and that stood us in good stead when we played. We played for each other and looked out for each other.

John Byrne

Keith and I were different players and it suited us both and worked so well. Where I brought more people into the game and held the ball up, as did Keith, he was raw and powerful and it worked to his advantage and he knew where the net was. He was frightening to watch on the pitch, I'm sure defenders were frightened of him and there were a few 'keepers who got clattered! We were the perfect foil for each other.

The championship season was just fantastic, there were a lot of highlights as we seemed to win nearly every game. The last game at home to Bury was something else. We beat them 3-0 in front of a crowd of over 8,000 and became the first team to get 100 points in a season. I remember the crowd streaming onto the pitch after the game and the celebrating. The team started celebrating early too. We still had one game left to play at Hereford, which we lost. We'd already achieved what we wanted to and the team were rather worse for wear for that game!

John Byrne

The team was full of good players, you can go through the team one by one, they were all stars, the likes of Roger Jones, a solid professional, and John MacPhail was a different class in defence.

The following season I wasn't playing as well. We'd lost at Bradford and I'd had a bad game and Denis Smith had a go at me. Afterwards I was told that Allen Mullary at QPR wanted to speak to me and Denis told me to get on a train to London. Viv Busby took me to the station and I went on the train by myself, and the deal was done. In someways it was a bit disappointing how that was handled but I have no bad feelings towards Denis or anyone at the club. In fact I played for Denis at other clubs and had some more successful times.

Bryan Foster was an absolute legend. He was there from the start when I signed as an apprentice and he was close to the apprentices with all the help we had to give him. His pitches were always magnificent.

He loved betting on the horses and I remember one day how he was riding on the table in the boardroom after his horse had won!

It was always a friendly, family club with great backroom staff. I can remember the likes of Shane Winship, George Teasdale, Maureen Leslie and Sheila Smith, all fantastic people. You were always made to feel welcome and still do when I've returned. The last time was in Steve Tutill's testimonial match against Middlesbrough. It was great to play there again.

I love the club and want them to do well and always look out for their scores every Saturday.

John Byrne

John MacPhail *(Centre-Half)*
1983-86 • 173 games • 29 goals
Division 4 Championship 1983-84
Clubman of the Year 1983-84 & 1984-85

When I knew York were first interested in me I didn't want to go there at first, I thought I could go to a club higher up. Denis Smith had watched me play twice without really seeing me play to my full potential but he still wanted to sign me. I knew Viv having played with him when he came on a loan spell at Sheffield United and it was these two that persuaded me to sign.

I learned a lot from Denis Smith, who was an outstanding defender, very aggressive and one of the bravest players I've seen. He would get sent off in every game these days!

Denis and Viv were great together, Denis would work with the defenders and Viv the forwards and we would try and kick the shit out of the forwards in practice matches!

The 1983-84 championship season was very special, being part of the first team to notch over 100 points in a season. Myself, John Byrne and Keith Walwyn in the divisional team of the year and then being crowned Clubman of the Year. It was such a big high.

The team that they put together knew each others strengths and weaknesses, were good players, worked for each other and had great team spirit, and thats why we were successful.

Things really changed at the club after the win over Arsenal in the F.A. Cup and the games with Liverpool, those were great money spinners for the club (not the players!) and a lot of facilities were updated in the ground.

There were some great characters at the club, Sean Haslegrave was a great bloke, and while Roger Jones was quite a placid man, there was me and Alan Hay, a couple of Jack the lads! Alan and I were like brothers, we went everywhere and did everything together. There were lots of pranks with team mates and one time after training when we were getting changed I put "Alzipan" in Alan Hay's knickers and when it kicked in he came in screaming as his bollocks were burning and red and he couldn't get rid of it!

Keith Walwyn was a little lamb off the pitch but when he went out to play he was very aggressive. He, along with Keith Houchen, had the worst dress sense of anyone I've known! Keith Houchen used to be known as "the man from C&A"! He got plenty of stick!

Alistair McClean is a pal of mine and he used to own Oscar's wine bar, and when we played Arsenal, he bet the team that he would give us 48 bottles of champagne if we beat them. As you will know, we won 1-0 and being a man of his word, gave the lads 48 bottles of champers. The thing is, myself and Alan Hay used to go to Oscar's at lunchtime as he would serve

"York City specials" and we managed to drink the majority of the bottles before the rest of the lads got there!

When we drew Liverpool in the next round he doubled his bet! 96 bottles of champagne, and we were leading 1-0 until very late on!!!

I wanted to stay at York, my girlfiend at the time, and

John MacPhail

now my wife, was from York and I was wanting a two year contract. Denis said that his hands were tied and could only offer me a years contract and no more. Terry Cooper at Bristol City came in and he offered me the two year deal I wanted and the transfer went to a tribunal. City wanted £50-60,000 and Denis took along clippings from the Arsenal and Liverpool games, details of my man of the match performances, but the York board wouldn't give me a two year deal and that swung the outcome. Bristol only had to pay City £13,000 and Denis flipped. I thought he was going to smack someone!

Some time later, I understand Denis wanted to re-sign me and I wanted to come back to York, but a week later Denis took the managers job at Sunderland so then I thought no more of it. Two or three weeks later Terry Cooper said that Denis Smith had called and wanted me at Sunderland. After the outbursts at the tribunal I hadn't been speaking to Denis. He told me to get the first train up to Sunderland. I'd just managed to get the right train to get up there, and the first thing that Denis said to me was "You're fucking late". I hadn't been to Roker Park before so I was shown round the ground with the chairman and Denis was able to offer me everything I needed, so I signed there and then on the day! Denis knew I could do a job for him, and in my first season with Sunderland I scored 17 goals and was second in the North East Player of the Year Award behind Paul Gascoigne!

John MacPhail

Keith Houchen *(Forward)*

1984-86 • 88 games • 27 goals
Division 4 Championship 1983-84

My first and most obvious memory of my time playing at York City would have to be making my debut in 1984 away at Aldershot signing just on the transfer deadline. I had been at Leyton Orient for 2 years after having signed for my first professional club Hartlepool United where I had burst on to the scene at 17 and had been expected to go onto great things after signing for Orient. This. however, had not been the case and I had endured a pretty miserable 2 years at a club which was on a downward curve when I arrived and was not the happiest place to be around and remained in terms of team spirit very poor.

What a difference I found on signing for York and travelling to that first match at Aldershot. The team had been top of the League (4th Division) all season and I was lucky enough to walk into the happiest and probably the most confident dressing rooms of any I ever played in. We won 4-1 that day and I made my debut coming on as a substitute after Steve Senior unfortunately broke his leg. I played in midfield for the first time in my career and absolutely loved what what was a pretty memorable debut, scoring in open play, missing a penalty and being booked!

Denis Smith and Viv Busby had brought together a tremendous squad of players and, as I said earlier, had created a wonderful morale and team spirit which was a pleasure to be part of.

John MacPhail, Ricky Sbragia, Gary Ford, Alan Hay, John Byrne, Keith Walwyn, Steve Senior, these are just some of the players which together had 3 or 4 great seasons and played in some memorable matches.

Arsenal at home in the F.A. Cup of course was a fabulous victory for the club and for the players, and of course on a personal note, it was for me my first taste of real acclaim and national publicity when I converted a penalty in the last minute of the ninety to help us claim a fabulous victory. As I remember that day, I have to say I will never forget the long wait that I had as the ref calmed and sorted all the protests from the Arsenal players, and the feeling of expectation that literally hung in the air as I waited on the edge of the box. Luckily I scored, but the way the crowd was that day I'm sure that they would have willed the ball in anyway.

There were many amusing stories from that time. We used to train at the mental hospital at Clifton and we did tend to see some very funny things ie people bursting out of bushes in pyjamas and joining in practice matches or the lady who used to stand there most weeks putting all the training balls into her bag to take back to her room. But probably the funniest thing was when we were all on a training exercise over at Guisbrough, we were staying at the Territorial Army barracks and were being put through some very hard work on the local hills. The first night in the dorm despite everybody being exhausted, most of the players were being a bit daft and loud in the darkness as footballers generally tend to do!! – laughing, making noises and throwing things around in the dark. Keith Walwyn, in particular, was getting pretty annoyed about this as he was desperate to get some sleep and eventually he erupted out of bed and screamed at everybody to be "Fucking quiet" just at the exact moment that Denis Smith and Viv Busby walked in and switched the light on. The sight of Keith who was 6ft 4 ins and very well hung, but who had a very high squeeky voice, stood in the middle of the room with his fists clenched at everybody sent the room into absolute hysterics.

I can honestly say that the time I spent at York City was amongst the happiest of the twenty years that I spent in the professional game.

Andy Leaning *(Goalkeeper)*
1985-87 • 86 games

My connections with York City start from the age of seven, my Dad, Frank, was a season ticket holder, and I attended my first game at Bootham Crescent back in 1970. From then on it was always an ambition of mine to represent the club at some level.

In 1977, at fourteen years of age, I signed schoolboy forms for Middlesbrough football club, being taken there by Jack Pinder, the ex-City player, who was scouting for them at the time. I shared the goalkeeping role for two years with Kelham O'Hanlon (currently assistant manager at Preston NE) and when Kelham, who is a year older than me, was offered an apprenticeship, it was then I was offered the same terms at York City. I declined the offer on my dad's advice, instead taking a joinery apprenticeship, whilst continuing to play for City's youth side. In our first season we reached the 1979 Northern Intermediate League Cup final losing 1-0 twice over two legs against the same Middlesbrough team I had left a year previous, also appearing in that side were John Byrne, Gary Ford and Steve Senior, who were to give City some excellent service in the coming years.

Barry Lyons, who was laying the foundations for York's youth policy, needed a goalkeeper on a more permanent basis than I could commit at the time, it was then that Mick Astbury joined the club leaving me to play locally for the next couple of years, firstly with York Railway Institute until Jim Collis asked me to play for Rowntree's in 1983. Quite by chance, towards the end of the 1985 season, City's reserves needed a keeper to play out the last few games of the season. Denis Smith rang and asked me to play, I never looked back being determined to take my chance a second time around.

Mick Astbury who was then first choice keeper, after City had released Roger Jones, suffered a facial injury at Bristol Rovers and I made my first team debut for York City on 4 November 1985, a 1-1 draw at Newport County. Ironically, the first goal I ever conceded in the League was an own goal from none other than Steve Senior, who in an attempt to play the ball back to me ended up putting it in the top right hand corner of the net. What a start to my professional career.

Three games stand out in my mind, firstly during the cup run of 85/86 - the two matches with Liverpool - particularly the game at Anfield where York were robbed of what would have been one of their greatest ever F.A. Cup results, a victory over the reigning European champions in their own back yard. People often ask me about that night and, to be honest, the only thing I can vividly remember is Keith Walwyn chasing a long ball through the middle, a collision with Grobbelaar, Hansen and Lawrenson, the ball ending up in the back of the net, the two sides lined up for a kick off only for the ref to eventually give a free kick. At the end of extra time, with Liverpool finishing 3-1 winners, I can remember Kenny Dalglish coming up and shaking my hand saying that we had been robbed over the two games, bearing in mind the debatable penalty given in the first game at Bootham Crescent. The Cup run that year was a great experience for everyone connected with the club, particularly for people like myself and Tony Canham, who scored the goal that night, both of us were playing non league football six months earlier, and I can still remember us both standing outside Denis Smith's office wondering if we would even be offered contracts the previous summer.

The other game I have fond memories of was the "derby" match with Middlesbrough on New Years Day 1986.

As we all gathered at the Royal York Hotel on New Year's Eve we were met with the news that due to heavy rain the game was 99.9% certain to be cancelled. As was customary during Denis and Viv's reign all the players met in the bar at 7.00pm for a half of lager or whatever you wanted to drink. The usual hand shakes wishing every one a Happy New Year took place, but with the news we had received earlier one half led to maybe two or three or four, as usual the curfew was 10.00 pm to be back in our rooms.

The next day due to the outstanding work of Bryan Foster the groundsman (a great character to have around the football club at the time, respected by all the staff and players, you could fill the pages of this book with stories about Bryan, who was sadly missed after his untimely death) the pitch was heavy but playable. After a good breakfast and a couple of glasses of water, we ended up putting on our best performance of the season being 2-0 up very quickly and running out 3-1 winners.

There is a saying in football that the club is only as good as it's senior pros, at that time there was a wealth of experience at the club, people like Ricky Sbragia, Malcolm Crosby, John MacPhail, Sean Haslegrave and Keith Walwyn kept the younger pros in check, we were no angels but generally we played and socialised as a team knowing where to draw the line, anyone stepping out of line would be told in no uncertain terms in-house.

Andy Leaning

The effect that Denis Smith and Viv Busby had over the players and on the team cannot be underestimated, it was arguably one of the most successful periods in the clubs history. In my opinion they were the perfect partnership. Make no mistake about it Denis was in charge, one of his favourite sayings was "I'll give you enough rope to hang yourself," but Viv's extra ordinary coaching and man management qualities helped everything run smoothly. I personally owe them both a great debt, firstly for the faith Denis showed in me as a player to sign me from non league, and the time spent by Viv on the training ground shaping me up, laying the foundations for me to carve out a 15 year playing career for myself.

I personally felt that team was split up too early, the turning point, in my opinion, was when City failed to agree terms with John MacPhail, who left to join Bristol City. The following season there was a mass exodus with the majority of players and management team leaving the club, mostly onto better things. All in all it was a sad end to one of the best chapters in the club's history, the profile of the club was high after a promotion season coupled with some good cup runs, with an attractive side playing regularly to gates of 5,000 people.

I have fond memories of my time spent as a player and a supporter of York City Football Club. I fulfiled my ambition to represent the city and it was a great honour to play in what were exciting times for the club.

Kevan Smith *(Centre Half)*
1988-89 • 33 games • 5 goals

I came from Coventry City, where we had won the F.A. Cup in 1987 and although I had a year and a half left to run on my contract, I asked for a transfer, due to lack of first team opportunities as John Sillet always reverted to the Peake-Kilcline partnership whenever possible.

On asking for a transfer I had quite a few options, Leyton Orient, Northampton, Reading, Hartlepool, Cambridge and of course York City. Being a northerner it could only be York a) because it was a nice club and place, one I had always admired from afar due to one of my best pals, Keith Houchen, filling me in with the finer details of the club and b) Hartlepool had no chance due to my six years with their deadly rivals Darlington – too many friends would have put my windows in!

So York it was. After meeting the manager Bobby Saxton, who was accompanied by a funny looking fella in a Post House Hotel just off the M1, it was just about signed, sealed and delivered that night.

I met the players in pre-season, when we went to Edinburgh University for 7 days. I immediately felt there was resentment to me by one or two players, due to where I had come from and the fact that I had a brand new car in the car park. They obviously thought I was some flash, big time Charlie, but they couldn't have been further from the truth.

Once the season got underway, things did not go as planned or hoped, and after a short while Bobby Saxton resigned. A few of us tried to dissuade Bobby but he was a very proud man and was not for turning. Thankfully, he went on to greater things with Sunderland and Peter Reid. Barry Swallow (Director) took over for a while and then eventually John Bird, with Alan Little as his number 2.

Now, don't get me wrong, I had a lot of time for "Birdie" as a person but not as a football manager. In my opinion, he was naive tactically and my idea of football was not to hit Row C everytime the ball was at one's feet, as John's was. Alan Little was far more football wise and, as time has now shown, was a great servant and manager to York City, who was eventually pooed on from a great height.

I really don't recall any fantastic matches when I played, but it must be said that York City never saw the best of Kevan Smith as a player. In my opinion there were certain factors, Bobby Saxton kept too many losers from his relegation side, just before I joined, and then all the unsettlement of managers didn't help, and John Bird being unsuitable.

I was 'forced' out after one season, with 2 more years to run on my contract, "Birdie" simply told me I would not play the following season.

To be honest, although very reluctant to go, he did me the biggest favour of my career, as I joined Brian Little back at Darlington, where I was made captain and we won the GM Vauxhall Conference and the 4th Division championship the following year.

I don't know of too many other players with other clubs interested who would go from what is now the Premiership to the Conference in one season. Brave or stupid? I'd like to think brave for the challenge!!

One funny moment, which will stay with me forever, involved our groundsman "Fozzie" Bryan Foster (the funny looking fella with Bobby Saxton when I signed). John Bird wanted us all training on the pitch on New Years Day which meant "Fozzie" opening the club up that morning. He was effing and blinding because he'd obviously been out drinking all night. Anyway, we reported for 10am and "Fozzie" was there as drunk as a skunk, so myself and Paul Johnson got him out of the way of "Birdie" and got him a coffee, and told him to sleep it off and after training we would come and wake him up. Off we went onto the for pitch training. At the end of training, "Birdie" sat us all in the centre circle and started chatting about the coming match with his back to the tunnel. As he was talking we could see "Fozzie" coming out of the tunnel, it looked as though he'd taken his shirt off. As he came out further we could see he was bollock naked with just a pair of wellies on and proceeded to have a piss on the edge of the pitch. We were absolutely pissing ourselves and trying to hold ourselves in. "Fozzie" gave his willy a shake, stuck two fingers up and disappeared back down the tunnel. By the time "Birdie" had turned round all you could see was this plume of steam rising up. To this day I don't think "Birdie" believed us but it was absolutely hilarious and will never be forgotten. Sadly, a few years later, "Fozzie" passed away. God Bless him.

In my opinion York City FC is still a lovely club with loyal supporters who I find and found to be nice and very friendly. I don't believe Alan Little should have been dismissed. Where have they gone since? They were in a transitional period when I was there and, in my opinion, are again.

I am pleased my career took me (although briefly) to York City and am pleased to still be in football as assistant manager at Hull City AFC.

Kevan Smith

Iain Dunn *(Forward)*
1988-91 • 89 games • 11 goals

I started playing for York professionally at the age of 18 in 1988. I had played regularly for the youth team, although I wasn't on the YTS Scheme. I had gone to study further education at York College and it was here that I got the chance to play for England under 19s (8 caps in total). This fact helped propel me into the thoughts of then manager Bobby Saxton. I played for the intermediates and reserves under Ricky Sbragia and he was inspirational in my getting offered a contract. I was looking forward to playing for Bobby as he really was a good coach (which he has since proved at Sunderland). Unfortunately Bobby resigned early on in the 88/89 season.

As it happened, on a personal note, things worked out for me as I was selected by new manager John Bird for his first game in charge. I think we were away to Grimsby. I played the last 20 minutes or so. I made my full debut in the next game, scoring against Doncaster.

I thought everything was going fine. I'd scored 3 goals in my first 5 games and all the stories of top clubs looking at me were materialising when inexplicably John Bird decided to drop me 'for my own good'. I'm sorry, but when an 18 year old comes into the fray and is scoring you don't stop the momentum. If an 18 year old starts off like that nowadays he is worth a million!

The person who stands out in my memory was Bryan Foster. Remember I was only young and this bloke seemed a right old nutter!! At first I was a little scared of him!! It turned out that he was a joker and used to have all the players in stitches with his stories and general behaviour! Mad!

Unfortunately my time at York wasn't really a success story! We were a struggling team filled with inexperience for the first year or so. We then signed David Longhurst and although I felt threatened by his arrival I soon realised I could learn from him. He really was a good player and a good signing. As it turned out I got on really well with him to the extent that we both enrolled on a French study course at York Technical College!! I had an 'O' level in French so I was just going to brush up on what I'd learned. I don't think "Longy" had done any before!! or maybe because he was older he had forgotten (all of it!!) It was hilarious for me because we had to introduce ourselves to the class (you were expected to know a bit) and unfortunately "Longy" was the first person. He just said "Hello, my name is David," he didn't realise it was meant to be in French!! He died a week later.

All the players were devastated that day. A little remembered fact was that I was the player who came on for "Longy" that day. I remember the night after it happened, me and my mate Simon Leaper, who had got close to "Longy" through regular drinking sessions at my brothers' Wine Bar, Oscars, just didn't know what to do. We went to Oscars every night and just talked about him. It was remarkable really, but I suppose you had to be there. The next time we played, guess who

Iain Dunn

took Longy's shirt? Me! I don't know if it had a long term bearing on my career or not but I do remember feeling some sort of pressure.

As I've said, my time at York was with a struggling team and I think the above events may have had a bearing on my career and I was released after just 3 years. This devastated me at the time but looking back it was for the best as I had a great time in football, culminating in signing for Huddersfield Town. I realised the difference in attitudes was on a totally different plateau and to get success you needed the right players with the right mentality. Something I believe John Ward brought to the club after I had gone. As a lifelong supporter of City I only want them to do well and was desperate for success with them and I feel gutted that in between the glory days of Denis Smith and John Ward I played in a very poor City team!

Iain Dunn

the *1990s*

Former Hartlepool boss John Bird was City's new manager and the teams League form picked up at first. The newly established trio of Steve Tutill, Andy McMillan and Wayne Hall as well as winger Tony Canham would all give the Club excellent service and would be rewarded with testimonials towards the end of the 80s.

City found themselves in the bottom 4 of Division 4 and the board took a gamble and appointed the unknown John Ward from the England coaching set-up to replace John Bird as manager during the 1991-92 season.

At first there was slight improvement but during the close season, Ward brought in Gary Swann, John Borthwick and equalled the club record to buy striker Paul Barnes from Stoke. What a transformation.

The team won their first 4 Leagues games (a new record) and won 8 of the first 9 games. The team were playing exciting football and they eventually finished 4th and in the play-offs. They beat Bury over the two legs to send the club to Wembley for the first time. They crowned a fabulous season with a penalty shoot-out win over Crewe, despite manager John Ward being poached by Bristol Rovers a few months earlier.

Alan Little led the team to the 3rd Division play-offs the following season but after narrowly missing out the team started to struggle and after several relegation battles City once again found themselves back in the basement.

Steve Tutill *(Centre Half)*
1988-98 • 366 games • 7 goals
Promotion 1992-93
Clubman of the Year 1990-91

Whilst at York City we were all given club blazers and trousers which we had to wear for matches home and away. It sounds ok doesn't it but there was one slight problem, the trousers were almost sky blue and the jackets were maroon in colour.

We were told Keith Usher (the club secretary) had chosen them and that Keith wasn't really colour blind.

The story gets better because at one particular away game I was stood in the hotel reception when I was approached by a particularly smart looking gentleman. He asked if I would take his bags up to his room and leave them outside his door. He then handed me a fiver and walked off. I couldn't stop laughing because he had mistaken me for a porter due to the lovely outfit I was wearing. I left his bags in reception and kept the fiver and bought myself a bottle of wine on the way home!

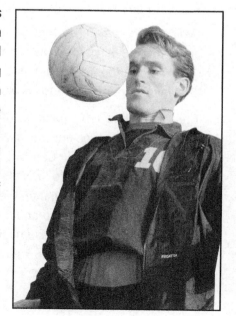

Andy McMillan *(Right Back)*

1987-99 • 492 games • 5 goals
Promotion 1992-93
Clubman of the Year 1995-96

During my playing career at York City I have had some very good partners on the right side. One of the best and many York City fans' favourite player was Jon McCarthy. He never gave up, chased everything, worked hard when attacking and defending. A player who always trained the way he played. There was also Greame Murty very similar to Jon – a good athlete who had tremendous potential and gave everything he had.

There were many fantastic occasions. The Play-off final against Crewe at Wembley is an obvious one. Wayne 'ginge' Hall scoring the decisive penalty. What a tremendous occasion, one that will never be forgotten. A chance to play at Wembley and win.

I will always remember Tony Canham telling all the players to enjoy the occasion. The night before he and his 'sidekick in crime' Nigel Pepper had a video camera and interviewed all the players. I would love to know where that tape went.

Then there was THAT game at Old Trafford in 1995. We were having a poor season and we were drawn against Manchester United in the Coca-Cola Cup. We travelled down for the game in the morning and got to the hotel for something to eat and to try and relax before the game. We spent it talking about trying to keep the result down to about seven giving us a chance in the return leg!!!!!! 3-0 to the mighty reds of City – one of the greatest shocks in football. I remember looking at the score board above our fans. I was sure I was dreaming.

I've been a Manchester United fan all my life and we went to Old Trafford and won! The return leg at Bootham Crescent saw the return of one of the greatest players ever to play for United, Eric Cantona. He made his first appearance away from Old Trafford since that famous karate kick at Crystal Palace. We lost 3-1 on the night but went through – an amazing night.

We had another amazing night when we played Everton at home also in the Worthington Cup. We had a tremendous 1-1 draw at Goodison Park and a fantastic 3-2 home win.

Thinking back to that game, I think that had to have been one of our finest performances all the time I was there.

I'd like to give a special mention to three managers at York City who all had a tremendous affect on my life. Bobby Saxton who gave me the chance to be a professional footballer. He was one of the nicest people you could ever wish to meet.

We went away to Scotland one year. He worked us to the ground during the day and afterwards all he said to us was to make sure we were back for training the next day. As you can imagine all the lads had a great time and training the next morning, as you could imagine, was poor!

John Ward was a fantastic coach and manager. He came into the club and totally transformed the team. He gave everyone the confidence and self belief to perform, told you never to worry about mistakes but to learn from them. I can never remember him raising his voice. It was such a shame when he left and a shame the board never tried harder to keep him.

I spent most of my playing career under Alan Little in one form or another. I had a lot of respect for him. He was desperate for York City to do well and he lived and breathed the club.

I would also like to take this opportunity to make a special mention to a very good friend of mine David Longhurst. It was a terrible tragedy for a player in his prime.

I will always remember about 20 of us going to Spain on an end of season trip. All David would play on the cassette player was "the Jam". By the end of the third day, having listened to it night and day, a few of us decided that we had had enough.

We buried it in the sand – probably still there to this day! He never knew what had happened to his beloved tape and for the rest of the holiday all we heard was him moaning that he couldn't find it. Know one had the heart to tell him what had happened to it. Many of the players still fondly remember him. What a character.

It was sad how it all ended at York. A fall out with the new manager and chairman. Never in my wildest dreams did I see it ending the way it did, having been told that I would have to sign for a particular club or I would be sacked. It goes to show how much loyalty counts at York City having spent 12 wonderful years there.

Jon McCarthy *(Winger/Forward)*
1990-95 • 233 games • 38 goals
Promotion 1992-93
Clubman of the Year 1991-92 & 1994-95

I was brought to the club by John Bird and Alan Little, who I had played for as a junior at Hartlepool United. Having being released by Hartlepool, because I chose to continue my studies at Nottingham Polytechnic, I was offered a chance to play for York reserves. This involved travelling from Nottingham by train to wherever the reserves were playing on a Wednesday night. I was very grateful for this second opportunity. Alan Little seemed to be the person who believed in me and thought I was worth a chance. He was my youth team coach at Hartlepool, my reserve team coach at York and ultimately my manager at York. Subsequently, he has been the biggest influence on my career, from whom I learnt all the basics of being a professional footballer and more importantly the attitude (principles of hard work and discipline).

My debut was an F.A.Cup tie against Darlington at Feethams. I travelled from Nottingham on Friday evening because the squad had injury problems. I thought I would be the 14th man but read in the paper at York that I would be playing. I was very nervous but in a good way that energised me. We earned a replay with a 0-0 draw but I should have have scored. I must have had three "one-on-ones" with their keeper in the first 20 minutes.

My home debut was the replay against Darlington. A great night in which we beat out local rivals. I remember how good it felt to be part of a successful dressing room, and the pre-match ritual of some players taking a swig out of a bottle of

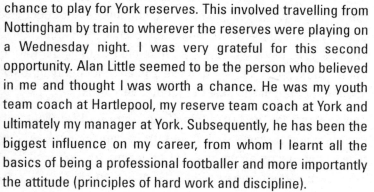

whisky before they ran out! And also the post match ritual of 24 cans of McEwans lager by the big bath! I will always remember the sight of Chris "Ged" Marples in the bath singing at the top of his voice with a can of lager in one hand and a cigarette in the other! I decided on a shower!!

I will always be grateful for the opportunity John Bird gave me. He was a very "hard" manager but honest and fair with it. He once came in at half-time after a bad performance and sent the FULL cups of tea flying around the dressing room. Then threw the tray on which they had once sat right across the room. The tray hit Paul Atkin on the shoulder and ricocheted onto my head. Some of the lads leapt to my defence but I was too scared to say anything as a "young lad". I think the gaffer got a shock, he was trying to make a point, not intending to hit anyone. Scared at the time but funny afterwards!

I also remember the crowd chanting "John Bird Out" outside the changing rooms the night before he got the sack. A sad time. I felt guilty about the gaffer losing his job and the uncertainty about who would be the new manager.

John Ward was an excellent appointment. A great coach to work with and his arrival totally changed the atmosphere at the club. His brand of man-management/psychology was very positive and rubbed off on everybody. He was able to deal with players, fans and the media and his signings turned a team which drew a lot of games into one which suddenly began to win regularly. His acquisition of Paul Barnes was instrumental in our success. Now we had another 25 goals a season. But arguably his greatest achievement was to get 15+ goals for the team by converting Ian "Blackie" Blackstone into a goalscoring left winger. John Ward laid the foundations for the season in which we gained promotion. It was no surprise that he was 'headhunted' for other jobs and eventually left.

I have a high regard for Alan Little, who enjoyed being the No. 2 at the club and was an excellent link between the players, with whom he was popular, and the manager. I think he rather reluctantly took the role as manager but the statistics would show that he was one of the clubs most successful managers: the clubs only visit to Wembley; promotion via the 3rd Division play-offs; getting to the play-offs the following year in Division 2; made profit on players; and the cup victories over Manchester United and Everton.

Following the departure of John Ward, the team could easily have faded but Alan was very astute in not changing too many things. He gradually put his influence on the team which provided the stability which allowed us to gain promotion that year, too much change could have affected us.

There are a couple of other games that stick out in my mind, one of them being the 5-1 victory at Barnet. This was our first

game after the departure of John Ward. An uncertain week for the club ended with one of the best performances of my time there. A totally dominant display capped off with a hat-trick by "Barney". I remember going over to the fans at the end of the game and the very happy bus on the long journey home!

And of course there was the Wembley play-off final. I have lots of memories like every York fan. The occasion really caught the imagination of the

City. Driving up to the stadium and seeing all the fans. The changing rooms, walking down the tunnel, the tension of the match itself. I had a chance to win the game in the last minute of normal time. I broke from a long way out, took on the last defender but blazed the shot over the bar. Fortunately I was able to score the first penalty and led the chase to catch "Ginner" after he had won the match for us!

There are a few people who I would like to give a special mention to.

My first sighting of the groundsman Bryan Foster was him chasing a first team player round the pitch with a pitchfork. I thought he must be a right old grump. But I soon learnt that it was just part of his act. Beneath this tough exterior was a very gentle, kind man who would do anything for you. He was very proud of his pitch and I caught him with tears in his eyes the day he got his suit to go to Wembley.

I remember the lads dragging him to "Silks" nightclub on his 50th birthday and he had a great time. I also have vivid recollections of him terrorising the bookmakers if his horse had lost! There was always a smell of fish & chips in the dressing room corridor on the occasions of night matches. It was "Fozzie's" tea if he had been there preparing the pitch all day.

Fozzie's sudden death was a very sad day for the club and the amount of people whose lives "Fozzie" had touched became apparent. A very popular man.

"Stocko", John Stockton, was always able to get you anything or point you in the right direction. He was a big mate of Shaun Reid and he took me under his wing when I got to the club. He made sure I got a good deal when I was buying my first car and would make sure I wasn't stuck in the digs getting bored on a Sunday afternoon!

Ian Blackstone was a breath of fresh air when he came to the club. He had worked all his life and played non-league football. He couldn't believe he was getting paid to play football professionally. He started work at 10am and was finished by 1pm and couldn't believe his luck. He was very laid back, called the gaffer by his first name and made the most of his time in football. A good player who was very important in the promotion winning season.

My last game for the club was a pre-season game versus Sunderland. Alan Little called me into his office after the game and gave me a piece of paper with John Rudge's phone number on it. The club had accepted a fee from Port Vale and I was to give them a call.

Jonathan McCarthy

Paul Stancliffe *(Centre Half)*

1991-94 • 103 games • 3 goals
Promotion 1992-93
Clubman of the Year 1992-93

During my time at York there were two outstanding matches which readily come to mind. The Coca-Cola 1st leg match versus Manchester United at Old Trafford in 1995 which we won 3-0 (not many teams win at Old Trafford at all, never mind 3-0) and the 3rd Division Play-off final at Wembley versus Crewe Alexandra in 1993 (it is surely every schoolboy's dream to play at Wembley).

However, of the two matches, I have chosen the Wembley play-off match which was a relatively easy decision to make due to the significance and special occasion of the day.

My recollection of the whole Wembley occasion are still as clear now as they were 8 years ago, the buildup, the day and the celebrations later.

In the week proceeding the game the city of York was buzzing with excitement as the expectations grew as the day got nearer. The player's preparations for the match were intense but they also had to cope with the additional pressures of daily radio and TV interviews which a lot of the younger players had never previously experienced. As club captain I obviously had more than my fair share of media involvement.

We also had the usual Wembley ritual which ALL clubs participate in and that is the measuring and fitting of club suits for the big day.

Once our preparations in York were completed we travelled down on the day before the game and stayed in a very pleasant hotel on the outskirts of London.

Normally coach journies to matches are tedious but necessary parts of a footballer's life – but not this one. On the one hand we had Nigel Pepper with a video camera doing player interviews with himself as cameraman and interviewer, and then there was Tony Canham who was trying (very trying!!!) to entertain everybody by singing James Brown's "I Feel Good". The only problem was that 'TC' only knew the first two lines of the chorus and after 3 or 4 renditions he was, not too politely, told to "put a sock in it".

When the big day arrived the realisation that I was actually going to play at the famous Wembley Stadium did not really hit me until the coach started the final leg of the journey up Wembley Way and I saw my family waving proudly.

On seeing the dressing room for the first time I remember thinking how big the room was inside and, although it was neatly empty, how it had a great aura which made it feel as if it was full.

It certainly was a sobering thought when I realised what famous and talented players had been in this room in the past and the famous occasions on which they had played.

They say that the players don't remember anything about the match on their first visit to Wembley but I must say I remember everything. This may have been because I was, let us be kind and say, into the twilight of my career, and this was not only going to be my first game at Wembley but also my last.

On the day everybody played well, both individually and as a team, and while most observers who were present on the day will always remember Dean Kiely's penalty save and Wayne Hall's winner in the penalty shoot-out, my lasting memory will be of leading the team as captain up the steps to the Royal Box to receive the winner's trophy.

Paul Stancliffe

Again, I remember recalling, as I had done in the dressing room, all the truly great players who had walked up those steps before me and how I was honoured to be following in their footsteps.

Having received the trophy we then did the customary photo-call on the pitch followed by a lap of honour to the York fans who had given us tremendous support throughout the match by easily outsinging the Crewe fans.

On arriving back in the dressing room we opened the bubbly and enjoyed out last remaining moments in the great stadium.

This continued on the coach journey back to York which seemed much shorter than the journey down.

The following day we toured York in an open-top bus in the pouring rain but nobody cared, whether on the bus or in the streets, where an estimated 100,000 people joined in the celebrations.

John Ward *(Manager)*
1991-93

After my appointment on November 5th 1991 I soon realised that I had taken on a big football job but had walked into a very friendly and close knit football club. Led by Mr Douglas Craig as chairman, the board were willing to be patient (thank goodness) and give their new manager a decent chance. After 6 months we finished fourth from bottom of the League and a big decision was made on me. Keep him or release him was on the agenda and I understand that Mr Craig was very influential in deciding to keep me on.

I am delighted to say that the following year the club were promoted as the football club moved forward. Alan Little, Ricky Sbragia and Jeff Miller were brilliant in their support and all had major roles in that promotion, indeed Alan was manager at the Wembley success as I had departed for Bristol Rovers in March that year.

Main players were Paul Stancliffe, captain and centre half who was outstanding in a mean defence. Dean Kiely in goal emerged as a very good young player. Paul Barnes, whose goalscoring along with Ian Blackstone, Jon McCarthy and John Borthwick at centre forward, provided a pacey and strong forward line. Hall, McMillan, Canham, Atkin and Bushell all had regular and consistent qualities to ensure York City's trip to Wembley.

It was a good decision from Mr Craig to give us all that memorable season!!

John Ward

Not all was wonderful and successful though. The club's mini bus, that transported our Youth players along the A64 to training, decided to open its back doors one day and spread out footballs and other training equipment all over the ring road. Thankfully our players managed to cling on to the vehicle and survive enabling them to clear the carriageway of York City gear. Our request for a new, rust-free bus met dubious response because of the cost but John Dodsworth managed to acquire a small runabout bus from Harrogate that with some paint and restoration was ours for about £3,000.

Duly painted in club colours and roadworthy our new transport became Alan Little's pride and joy, departing Bootham at 10.00am every day at the ring of his bell! We often had local residents arms aloft expecting us to pick them up on the way round to town we looked that good!

Paul Barnes *(Forward)*

1992-96 • 179 games • 85 goals
Promotion 1992-93
Clubman of the Year 1993-94

When I signed for York it was my chance to play regular first team football. I spoke to John Ward and he said that this would be my chance to prove myself. I was scoring goals for fun in Stoke's reserves but needed the chance to prove to myself I could do it at first team level.

I came to York and saw what a lovely place it was, a lovely city and a great little club.

The team that John had put together was the basis of a good side which was just lacking a recognised goalscorer. The majority of the team were all quite young and at the start of their careers, Jon McCarthy, Andy McMillan, Steve Tutill, Nigel Pepper and Dean Kiely and we had a great first season together. John Ward brought in Gary Swann who brought his experience to a young side and everything just gelled together from the start. It was a young, pacey and skillful team and there was a great buzz in the dressing room. I remember the opening game of the 92-93 season, winning 2-0 against Shrewsbury, and then setting a club record by winning the first 4 league games on the trot. It was great for the crowds too, we were getting 3-4000 crowds regularly during the season.

At the end of my first season we got to the third division play-offs, a remarkable achievement. We drew the first leg 0-0 at Bury and Dean Kiely performed unbelievable heroics to keep the scores level. Then there was the full house for the return leg and Gary Swann scoring the winner to send us to Wembley.

The buzz around the city was just fantastic. I've got lots of memories of that day, not only of the game itself but the occasion as well. Laying on the ball for Swanny to score the goal, the penalty shoot out, the ribbing we gave Steve Tutill for giving away the penalty in the last minute – doing Superman impressions – and seeing my family in the stands, and also the rain as it poured down on the open top bus tour of the city the following day! It certainly put the players and the club into the limelight.

The following season was another great season, up a division and again reaching the play offs, but eventually losing out to Stockport County. I remember missing a good header from an Ian Blackstone cross before Stockport scored their winner.

In my opinion the club never strengthened the side when we were pushing for a place in the first division and never used some of the money the club had collected from big money transfers to buy some new faces. Maybe things would have been different and the club might not be where they are now.

The cup games against Manchester United in 1995 held lots of great memories. We were driving up to Old Trafford on the coach for the 1st leg and we were joking amongst ourselves what the score might be, and there were United fans outside on the pavement laughing at us. But what a night! I remember at the end of the game looking up at the scoreboard and it reading "United 0 York 3" a truly unbelievable night.

This result, of course, brought a lot of media attention and we had SKY TV knocking on our doors wanting interviews and I was glad it was only for a few days! I can imagine what the likes of David Beckham have to go through with the constant media attention they receive.

The next game was at home against Walsall and I remember scoring the winner and also the terrific reception we got from the crowd.

The return leg at Bootham Crescent against Man Utd was another big occasion, with the likes of Schmeichel and Keane playing and Cantona making his comeback. The Press were sat lined up all along the touchline. Before the game a guy from Puma offered me £500 a goal if I wore his boots. To this day I'm still not sure who got the final touch between Scott Jordan and myself for the winning goal. He told me he would pay me half the amount for now and we could sort it out later!!

I sometimes think that those games against Manchester United were better than the Wembley game because of its one off nature.

After my dispute with Douglas Craig I felt it was time to move on. I have no sourness towards him, I've met him a couple of times since and shook his hand. I had a great time at York and would recommend anyone else to go there. It's a terrific family club and there was a lot of spirit amongst the players, the likes of Nigel Pepper, Chris Marples and Tony Canham.

There were some differences in personality between John Ward and Alan Little, John was a good coach and great at man management whilst Alan was a good motivator and each approached the game very differently.

One thing I found was a major difference moving from York to a club such as Birmingham is the expectation levels of the fans. It's a big footballing city and the stakes are so much higher for them and expect so much more. You also get fewer chances for scoring so therefore have to be more clinical to be successful.

Paul Barnes

There were lots of characters at the club such as Nigel Pepper, Chris Marples, and Tony Canham but I have to give a special mention to the groundsman Bryan Foster. What a legend!! He was an expert pitch fork thrower and if you trod on his turf one would be flying through the air towards your head – and we wasn't trying to miss either!

He always joined in with the lads' nights outs, once turning up at Silks nightclub in his wellies, and there was one time he came into a bookies and started to tear off all the paper from the walls saying, "I'll do you all a favour."

I thoroughly enjoyed my time at York and would recommend the club to anyone.

Paul Barnes

Gary Swann *(Midfield)*
1992-94 • 100 games • 6 goals
Promotion 1992-93

I have been thinking of some stories when I was with City in the 92-94 seasons, especially at Wembley. Scoring the diving header in the play-off semi-finals against Bury to take City to Wembley was brilliant and the players in the dressing room before the match were telling me this is the time to score your first goal for the club, and what a time it was.

The most memorable match of my time at York City, and also of my professional footballing career, was playing at Wembley as the only York born player to score there. Seeing your name on the electronic scoreboard after you have just scored is fantastic and every footballers dream. A very proud moment for my family, friends and myself.

Two diabetics at Wembley

Being a diabetic and a diabetic footballer, similar to Gary Mabbut of Tottenham, you have to be disciplined in your fitness/health/diet routine to ensure correct blood sugar levels are maintained whilst playing and training. I had to treat the Wembley game slightly differently because of the big pitch and spongy grass, which can absorb more fitness energy than normal. Everything was fine until the 90 minutes was up and 30 minutes of extra time was to be played, I started to feel the early warning signs of my low blood sugar and ate a few dextrose sweets with some fluid. "Pep" (Nigel Pepper) my midfield partner came over to speak to me, I thought he might be wanting to talk about the tactics we could use to win the game but no. He said he was feeling knackered and could he have some dextrose sweets, which was no problem. The game carried on and I scored, they equalised and it went to penalties, which we won.

After the game we were celebrating in the dressing room, when "Pep" came over and said "Swanny, I'm still feeling knackered," I said "Have a couple more sweets and see Jeff the physio in a minute." He saw Jeff but thought it might just be the exhaustion of the match. Then we left to celebrate. During the next couple of days "Pep" was still not feeling well and went to see the club doctor and was diagnosed as diabetic. He was shaken, could not take it in and rang me to tell me his condition. We discussed the condition, its effects, the immediate and future treatment and how you control it and how it does not control you or your life.

"Peps" isn't the most disciplined player or person and found it hard going especially injecting the needles. It's quite ironic that he was the one who would take the piss and move away from me when I was injecting myself coming back from away games on the team coach, he always said he would never do that. That's why there were two diabetics playing at Wembley that day.

City player arrested at the ground

Paul Barnes, Darren Tilley and myself used to share cars to the training ground in New Earswick and on this occasion it was Darren's turn. On the way back from training one day there was a queue on one of the one-way streets near Rowntrees, so Darren took it upon himself to drive up on two wheels on the pavement to get to the front of the queue, clipping a couple of wing mirrors on the way. When he got to the front, to the sound of car horns beeping at us, he realised he could only turn left and he wanted to go right. He wheel span the car into the traffic as quick as he could just as a police car was going the other way. "Barnsey" said "did you see that police car Daz?" "Daz" said that he hadn't and I said " I think he's turning around and coming after you Daz" but Daz drove quickly back to the ground.

"Barnsey" and I told the other lads what he'd done and we started to take the piss saying that the cops had got the registration number of his car and will send a fine to him, but Darren was a little too cocky and said that no one would catch him.

"Barnsey" and I thought he might need bringing down a peg or two just to keep his feet on the ground. It just so happened that the club secretary Keith used to be high up in the police force and still knew a few people in the force, namely the local sergeant. We both told Keith the story, details of Darren's car and he thought it was worth pursuing and contacted his mate. A couple of days went by and Keith told us it was all arranged for after training the next day. We told the coaches, physio, players and apprentices to be in the tea-room after training. The gaffer and Keith told Darren to meet them after training in the office about a complaint that a motorist had made and the police wanted to interview him. The sergeant grilled him for over 30 minutes, with Darren frequently being heard apologising, and gave him a fine to pay with a discount if he paid it there and then. Darren said that he thought he had done nothing wrong and if he had he would pay the fine. The office has a door to the tea-room and all the staff were listening. As he started to get his wallet out, the door of the tea-room burst open and all the staff burst in laughing theirs heads off and saying it had served him right for being so cocky about it. Darren went bright red and swore he'd get his revenge on "Barnsey" and me.

Paddy Atkinson *(Left-Back)*
1995-98 • 50 games • 0 goals

I would just like to mention before you read the following that I dedicate my views in this book to a lovely and likeable man who all the players respected. Gerry Davitt a local businessman from Naburn, who attended all of the away games in his aeroplane and never missed a home game. He always invited the players to his house and helped them whenever he could, i.e. picking them up from the station, offering financial advice, etc. All the players attended his funeral and were devastated, especially as Gerry had just become a significant shareholder of the club.

My time at York City was very entertaining as the players were a varied and mixed bunch, but we had a very good team spirit with some interesting characters. I only wish the club had the ambition and drive that the players and manager did then, instead of apparently thinking about finances first.

All the players had the upmost respect for Alan Little (I had time for Alan myself). He was an excellent coach, but as manager he failed because I don't believe that he would stand up with his own views before the board. Eventually he did, with the fate of getting sacked.

We had a good squad at the time and in my final season we got as high as 3rd in the 2nd Division. We were crying out for 3 or 4 players to help drive towards promotion but no matter how hard Alan Little tried to bring in players he could not sign them. There were times when Alan would watch a player for 6 weeks, invite him for talks with his agent, only for the board to feel unable to meet the players' demands. What's the point in

Alan looking at players and I am sure it must have crossed his mind if the board were unable to break the wage structure which is, I believe, still in place now. There was a time when we couldn't attract part-time Conference players never mind a full time player because of the wage structures.

The squad stuck together but because of injuries and suspension the league position slipped eventually finishing 2nd or 3rd from the relegation zone.

Alan Little and his family were under huge pressure especially as he lived in York, apparently his daughter got bombarded at school with eggs, which is not right because at the end of the day it is only a game. Alan was in the firing line for others – those who made the financial decisions. The players used to get the same question asked from fans. "Where has all the money gone from the sales of Jon McCarthy, Paul Barnes, Nigel Pepper, Dean Kiely, Jonothan Greening and Richard Cresswell?" In the end we all started to wonder.

We did have the players to get promoted but I believe that we did not have the right directors. When it came to money issues the players were always having to fight for things like boots, tracksuits, new contracts, even pre-match meals (an essential part of a players diet before games). According to the directors the club would only pay for pre-match meals on journeys over 2 hours. I remember Burnley away takes 2 hours 15 minutes but we still did not qualify for a pre-match meal! The players could not believe how tight they were. The club once even refused Kevin Keegan 4 complimentary tickets for a game and said the normal allocation was only 2. Kevin Keegan told them to forget it and not to expect any favours from Newcastle in the future. Steve Tutill asked Newcastle for a testimonial but they declined. I wonder why? Middlesbrough kindly obliged.

Paul Stephenson was known for voicing his opinions to one and all and I think that is what sealed his fate at York. As he left, the papers quoted that Paul was the wrong side of 30 but they signed Neil Thompson at 33 so he must have been the right side of 33! When you look back the club never ever replaced Paul Stephenson and I don't think you ever could. Other players followed him out. Tony Barrass – as the club would not break the wage structure to keep him. Graeme Murty, Steve Bushell, Nigel Pepper, Paul Barnes, Richard Cresswell, Jonothan Greening and Alan Pouton all left for the same reasons. I feel sorry for all the players who had testimonials at the club as each one was released after their testimonials, Tony Canham, Steve Tutill, Andy McMillan and Wayne Hall. How can you do that to a long servant of the club? You can see from the above that the club really did lack ambition as money made from sale of players must have been used to finance the club.

The fans at York were good away supporters. We always had a contingency of fans travel near or far and make a lot of noise at places like Burnley, Preston, Bristol City and Wigan. It always seemed to be the same faces and they deserve a mention in this book for their loyalty. The noise they made was terrific. Even when we arrived back in the early hours of the morning there was always one or two hanging around the ground I always remember a fan called James who was always at the ground to meet the team coach no matter what time it was. I will remember the away support at Brighton when we had to win the game to stay in the 2nd Division after the season had finished. The scenes afterwards were amazing.

Paddy Atkinson

However, the home support had to be described as "interesting". There appeared to be a minority of fans who turned up only to give some players a barrage of stick. Gary Bull received a lot of stick for the lack of goals off the same one guy and a few other fans had to tell him to get off his back or don't attend the games. I also remember Tony Barrass, Nigel Pepper and Alan Pouton pointing the finger at certain individuals during a game and telling them to "shut it". It is not very nice playing at home under those circumstances, you get enough stick from away fans and no matter how bad the performance you should always get behind your team. Saying that I don't blame the fans as they only want success and if people behind the scenes appear to have the funds but are not spending wisely the performances will always be average.

The crowds at Bootham Crescent were always good when we attacked the David Longhurst stand as we seemed to attack that end better in games.

There was nothing better than to see a full house at Bootham Crescent getting behind the team. There was always a capacity crowd for a big Cup draw so where do these people go week in week out? I was working for Minster FM and I was asked how we could attract more fans. I suggested taking a leaf out of Watford's book giving free tickets to schools, as the kids would also have to attend with a family member. Once again the idea was declined by the board.

I would give the away support 10 out of 10 but the home support only 6.

I know there were some good cup runs during my time but the two fixtures which stick in my mind were the two games away at Brighton. I remember the first game, Paul Stephenson, Gary

Bull and I went for a walk at about 11 am. We decided to go to the bookies to put a bet on a horse and it was packed with different football supporters. We had our York City tracksuits on and three skinheads asked us if we were playing today. We told them we hadn't been picked yet and they said that it didn't matter anyway because there was not going to be any game played today that day. They continued to tell us that "when the big clock strikes 12 minutes into the game the pitch will be invaded and the goals ripped down in protest to the club being relegated and the ground sold". We didn't believe them as football had so many new security measures and we went back to the hotel not thinking any more of it as you normally get stick like that from home fans when playing away.

I remember the day clearly, we arrived at the ground and some fans had broken in the night before and pored broken glass on the pitch and sprayed "Sack the Board" in big black letters on the turf. The temperature down there was absolutely red-hot, well into the 80's.

We started the game well and could have scored twice in the opening minutes, then I remember going for a throw in and noticed a West Ham shirt. I thought it was a bit strange and then I remembered the conversation in the bookies. A crowd of 14-16,000 was a bit odd for a 2nd Division fixture especially as Brighton had been relegated. The next thing I know Paul Stephenson ran past me shouting "Leg it Paddy." I could not believe what I was seeing, thousands of fans pouring onto the pitch running towards the tunnel. There is a phrase "Shit off a stick" well that was me! We were locked in the dressing room by the police and warned it might get nasty. Nasty? This was a football match and all you could hear was the chants of the

Paddy Atkinson

fans and the banging of wood trying to get into the stand. The police were running too and fro with riot gear on.

As we left the ground in the team coach, fans were throwing bricks at us as if we were crossing a picket line. It was only afterwards we realised the extent of the damage, goals ripped down etc.

In the replayed encounter against Brighton, supposedly behind closed doors after the season had finished, City had to win or score two goals to stay up. Once again it was 80°+ but the pressure was intense to win the game. Carlisle had won on the Saturday and awaited our result to see if they would be relegated. They allowed 3,000 Brighton fans into the ground and 1,000 York fans but it sounded like 10,000 during the game. Their support was fantastic.

We played well but Maskell scored a screamer 5 minutes from half-time curling the ball past Dean Kiely from 25 yards. Alan Little did not say anything at half time. You could have heard a pin drop. We went out in the second half and trounced them. I had shared a room on all away games with Paul Stephenson and kept on at him that when he cut inside on his right foot he should not blast the ball but curl it and he would score. What a game to cut inside and curl a ball into the far corner. Then up popped Gary Bull two minutes later to score. The players and the supporters were ecstatic. There were scenes I will always remember. We had scored the two goals we needed to stay up, and just to rub it in Scott Jordan scored a third to win 3-1 and secure safety. The fans were singing as if they had won the FA Cup and the players were celebrating. Marvellous scenes.

My best friends at the club were Paul Stephenson, Gary Bull, Neil Tolson and Alan Pouton (who lived at my house). I was like

Paddy Atkinson

a big brother for Alan and nothing has changed as he is always at my house now. Paul Stephenson had a body swerve that could move a whole defence, Gary Bull was the coolest person at the club, nothing bothered him, Neil Tolson was the worst dressed person I know and Alan is so thick he was immediately instated with the nickname of "Trigger", the character from "Only Fools & Horses".

Alan Little read the riot act one day as he was disappointed no players had attended a church service for the club chaplain one particular Sunday. He stormed into the dressing room and said no player would be allowed time off for any appointments because of this. You could have cut the atmosphere with a knife when he left the dressing room, Alan Pouton said that he didn't know why he had to go to church because he wasn't even religious. One of the players asked what religion he was and Alan replied "I think I am Aquarius, Church of England."

I used to be the brains behind a lot of pranks and there was a time Alan Pouton got off with a girl on a night out and the lads wound him up about catching something. We always got weighed on a Friday morning before training so I told the physio who recorded the weights to tell Alan that he had lost 6 pounds. This went on for four weeks and Alan started to get worried. I had to tell him the truth in case his performances suffered!

Gerry Davitt had a small 6-seater aeroplane which he used to fly to away games with his friends. Alan Pouton was injured for the Watford away fixture but asked Gerry if he could travel in his aeroplane. Gerry told Alan "the plane is full mate," so Alan replied "I don't mind Gerry, I'll just sit in the aisle." When everyone heard Alan's reply they fell about laughing. I think Alan thought the plane was a Boeing 747!!! This was one of Gerry's favourite stories and told everybody as he loved the players at York City.

Tony Barrass *(Centre Half)*
1994-99 • 210 games • 15 goals
Clubman of the Year 1996-97

My time at York was very important to me in so many ways, firstly it was Alan Little who brought me to York, who I think was a good manager. But most of all it was the times when we played the likes of Manchester United and Everton. Yes, scoring against Manchester United is the best part of my footballing career and always will be.

At my time at York there were some great lads such as Gary Himsworth, Steve Tutill, Gary Bull, Paul Stephenson and plenty more. Lets not forget Alan Pouton. He was a star on and off the pitch. I remember one time when I was injured and so I missed the lads trip abroad but I will always remember this. The lads were on the plane when "Pouts" was moaning about his ears hurting, so one of the lads said hold your nose and blow, so "Pouts" held his nose and blew. The lads were falling about laughing – he only held his nose and literally blew without holding the air in.

I wish everyone involved with the club, players and supporters, and all the people in the offices, all the best.

Bryan Foster

Printed in Great Britain
by Amazon

23530177R00059